Wear That Crown, Girl

God wants you to *thrive* in your singleness
season instead of waiting for a man to make
you happy or fill all your needs.

Anna Pavlov

TRILOGY CHRISTIAN PUBLISHERS
TUSTIN, CA

Trilogy Christian Publishers
A Wholly Owned Subsidiary of Trinity Broadcasting Network
2442 Michelle Drive
Tustin, CA 92780

For information, address Trilogy Christian Publishing

Rights Department, 2442 Michelle Drive, Tustin, Ca 92780.

Trilogy Christian Publishing/ TBN and colophon are trademarks of Trinity Broadcasting Network.

For information about special discounts for bulk purchases, please contact Trilogy Christian Publishing.

Manufactured in the United States of America

Trilogy Disclaimer: The views and content expressed in this book are those of the author and may not necessarily reflect the views and doctrine of Trilogy Christian Publishing or the Trinity Broadcasting Network.

10 9 8 7 6 5 4 3 2 1

Library of Congress Cataloging-in-Publication Data is available.

ISBN 978-1-63769-330-8

ISBN 978-1-63769-331-5 (ebook)

Contents

Dedication

Wear That Crown, Girl is an encouraging book that is relatable to all the singles out there. It is filled with raw stories, testimonies, and struggles for singles. It provides the space to relate and find encouragement in their singleness season. The book was inspired by the Lord, and I felt the Father's heart for the ladies as I was writing the book. The Father wanted the ladies to know that they are created *by God* and *for God* that has amazing plans for them, and He wants to reveal His plans and identify their worth to them.

Foreword

"God instructs husbands in 1 Peter 3:7 (NLT) to honor and treat your wives with understanding. Anna Pavlov's voice as a woman and therapist shines brightly throughout the pages of *Wear that Crown, Girl*. Her book is a must-read for both women and men. For men, it will unlock some of the mysteries of the woman's mind, allowing us to better understand them. Anna's transparency and journey will inspire any woman who reads it and enlighten every man seeking to understand the women in their lives better."

Jonnathan Zin Truong
Author of *Buddhists, Mormons & Jesus*

"As a woman who met and married her husband in her thirties, I related to emotions, thoughts, and the turmoil of Anna's story. Throughout her book, Anna beautifully paints her story like an artist on a canvas, using her life and experience to provide Godly wisdom to single women of any age desiring to be married. I love the boldness of how Anna shares her journey of how she has navigated singlehood and the pressures from culture and family to be married. This book is a must-read for all women, single or married. You'll laugh, you'll cry, and you'll be blessed."

Olivia Landes Truong
Pastor of God Manifest Church

"Anna Pavlov navigates the ups and downs of singleness, the dating process, and full surrender in her powerful and encouraging book Wear That Crown, Girl. Anna's book is filled with nuggets of wisdom from God's Word and her own personal experiences. She beautifully and candidly shares her heart, her testimony, and her intimate journey with the Lord. Anna's love for the Word of God and her trust in His timing are refreshing! Through personal stories and powerful encounters with her Heavenly Father, Anna expresses her deep gratitude to the Lord for His ever-present love, His Word, and His perfect timing. She counsels those who are tempted to "settle for crumbs" in their relationships to "invite Him (Jesus) into your heart and allow Him to pour out His love upon you." Anna shares that "If you find yourself changing for another person (in a negative sense), know that this is not from the Lord." Her book also includes carefully thought-out reflection questions at the end of each chapter, and powerful prayers are sprinkled throughout."

Deanna Millsap

My Testimony

Growing up, I was always the girl who would have a crush on a cute boy. You know the type of crush where you daydream about them every second, where you fantasize about getting together, getting married, and living happily ever after, just like couples do in Disney movies? I'm sure I'm not the only one who has these types of fantasies.

My family moved to the United States from Russia when I was three years old. And when we moved to the States, we settled in a predominately Russian/Ukrainian community. I grew up in a Christian home, mostly Pentecostal. My dad was a pastor until I was nineteen years old. So, I was pretty much at church all the time. My friends and I would attend church on Sundays religiously, more so because our parents made us attend, as opposed to us wanting to attend. While at church, the other girls and I would talk about the boys and who was into them from the youth group. Back then, that was what our world was about.

I recall during my teenage years, my crush called me, and I was on cloud nine. I couldn't even speak, I couldn't even think. It was like one of those scenes in the movies where someone's crush approaches them. They are in such shock that their brain freezes, and they forget how to speak. Ha! That was me when I spoke to my crush on the phone. However, because I was still young and was not thinking about getting married, I did not get to date my crush. I barely knew how to cook or even how to talk back then, let alone how to be married and start a family. Throughout my childhood, I lived in fantasy land and not reality. In the Slavic community, people are expected to get married early; that was the thing back then. So, after thinking everything over, I decided that I did not want to get married young and have children. I knew that eventually, I would want to get married and start a family, but not until I was much older.

But as I grew up, my best friend started dating a guy with the intention of getting married, just like most of the people did in our community. At twenty-one years old, I began thinking about where I was headed in life. The people around me seemed to have a direction or vision of being a lawyer, a doctor, or getting married and becoming a stay-at-home mom. However, I was not dating anyone or had anything serious going on, so I prayed to God and asked Him, "Where do I belong in this world?" Afterward, I would just sit there and wonder if I belonged anywhere in God's plan. It was new for me to pray to God and wait to hear Him speak. I was taught that God wants a personal relationship with His children, and so I decided to give it a try.

Then, one day, I was at work, and I heard the Lord speak to my heart (not in an audible voice), in a small, still voice, "Anna, you're not going to get married early, you're beautiful, and you're able to walk this plan out." When the Lord gave me those words, I was thinking that He meant I wouldn't get married before I was twenty-four age; otherwise, you were considered an old maid. Little did I know that His definition of "early" was different than what I imagined. If He would've clarified His definition of "early" back then, I think I would've died on the spot. Just kidding! I would have certainly protested that word. Luckily, back then, I just accepted it as, "Well, if it happens, then it's the Lord, and He has a plan for my life, so let it be. And if not, then, oh well, nothing's lost."

After accepting God's Word over me, I went on with my life. I graduated from college and got a full-time job that paid decently. I ended up not continuing in education because my grades were not great, so I worked full time and got into the ministry of leading a small group of teenage girls—not because I wanted to, but because it worked out that way. It was during that time that I discovered that I was good at listening and enjoyed counseling and ministry. Fast forward to the year 2019, I completed my master's degree in Marriage and Family Therapy and have been working in the field for a few years and can testify that God's hand was with me throughout those years. From the testimony of how I got through schooling to the breakthroughs that I witnessed in my sessions and my calling coming into existence, I can testify of God's faithfulness and goodness. Life has been amazing, filled with adventures, surprises, miracles, and of course, pain and suffering. What a good Father God is, that He knows the plans He has for us and what He created us for. And even when we don't obey Him, He remains faithful and uses everything, even our mistakes and wrong turns, for our good (Romans 8:28, MSG).

There's nothing insignificant about you. There is a reason for the way you are designed, the passions that He gave you, the desires in your heart, and the dreams that fill your mind. The Lord wants to partner with you and meet you where you are. You are precious in His sight, and He delights to meet with you. We all have a unique story and a unique calling. In this book, I hope to inspire you to dream big, follow Christ, and encourage you to step out into all that He has called you to for His glory.

Trust

The lens through how we see God and ourselves determines our destination. Similarly, faith drives our actions and our words according to the measure of grace that we are given.

When we know the Father's heart, we can trust that He is a good Father, and His plans for us are good. His plans are for us, to prosper us and bring us hope and a future (Jeremiah 29:11). When we truly trust Him, then we can trust Him with our future, our present, and our past. He is a God of justice, He is a God of redemption, He is a God of mercy. Our perspective matters because it impacts our outlook on life. If our perspective is tainted with betrayal, disappointment, or whatever else that we have in our hearts that needs healing, it can overshadow the good with the bad. Therefore, we need the Holy Spirit to come into our hearts and clean us, heal us, and restore us.

I confess that I didn't always believe God's promises or words. There were many days where I was confused, lost, bereft of all hope, and was convinced I was crazy. However, through many encounters with the Lord and His Holy Spirit, I found hope and love as He began healing me and transforming my life. All glory belongs to Him. I wish I could say, "I was always obedient to the Lord!" But I can't. However, I am convinced that through my journey, I have come to know the Lord better through encountering His amazing grace. It's amazing how through suffering, pain, and struggles, we get to know Him so much more intimately. In a beautiful exchange, He gives us beauty for ashes and joy for our sadness (Isaiah 61:3).

When I turned twenty-six, my parents started freaking out that I was still unmarried. They wanted me to get married because, as previously stated, it is expected in our culture that we marry at the age of twenty-six. They tried to suggest that I get married to one of the single men in our churches. I was not interested in that at all but felt bad because I loved my parents and wanted to please them. My parents really tried to help me get married. At that time, I felt as though my whole identity was wrapped up around getting married as if there were something obviously wrong with me because I was still single. Thank God I was able to see and understand that wasn't true. The truth is that sometimes, God calls people to marry when they're very young. Other times, He has a different plan. Just like the apostle Paul wrote in the Bible about how some people are meant to be married, and some people are meant to be single. Very few people can remain single, but I believe that there's a divine timing for everyone, especially if they are believers and truly praying about it.

Reflection Questions:

- What situations have impacted you and your trust with the Lord?
- Are there any areas of your heart that you need to trust the Lord with? (Finances, healing, provision, health, spouse, etc.)

How Culture and Our Environment Play a Role

When I started showing lines or wrinkles on my forehead, my dad pointed it out one day and suggested I might want to consider getting cosmetic work or surgery. It didn't offend me because I knew my dad and mom loved me, and that is how they were raised. They thought it was normal to point out people's imperfections and help them get help and that if I needed surgery, I should take advantage of it. They were good parents, and they meant well, but when there's a cultural component to our beliefs, it is ingrained in us, so they thought it was normal to get things "fixed" on our bodies. There's nothing wrong with make-up or getting some work done on your body or face. However, cosmetic surgery will not fix or heal the root of the issue but would just be masking the underlying issue or applying a Band-Aid.

When we are in the world, we can begin to mimic it, and it can leave us feeling empty inside, as if we are only defined by our looks and material possessions. That was how I used to feel growing up, and I began to feel insecure. First, I was not married by the standards and timeline of my culture, and now there were things wrong with my looks, making me feel that I was not good enough. I knew my parents would never intentionally try to make me feel insecure, but that's how I internalized it. So, I grew a little insecure in my identity. I felt like I needed to focus on my looks all the time; otherwise, people, especially men, were not going to see my worth.

The Lord met me in my despair, and He began to heal and restore all of the wrong mindsets, strongholds, and belief systems. For example, I believed, "I wouldn't be happy unless I was married," or "I need to look a certain way to attract men," and "I am not valued if I don't possess physical beauty." He began this transformation in me by allowing me to be in His presence. Suddenly, I would be so overcome by the Holy Spirit at church, during worship, during preaching, at home, or while reading His Word. As He began revealing His Word to me, He told me, "I am going to build your foundation." Back then, I didn't know what that meant, other than it

was something positive. As I write this, I begin to weep
tears of joy and praise Him because I didn't know how
broken I was or how much I needed His healing touch.
I began reading and studying the Word because God
told me that I needed to, as I would be teaching others.
I started meditating on His Word daily and believing it.
Eventually, His Word became part of me as it renewed
my mind (Romans 12:2), transforming me into a new
creation through Him over time. He began showing me
my identity and that I am beautiful without makeup
and without anything external. He began teaching me
that we are more than our clothes and looks and that
He truly looks at our hearts. He taught me that there
are other things in this world that are more important:
"But seek first his kingdom and his righteousness, and
all these things will be given to you as well" (Matthew
6:33). He began pouring out His love on me, and speaking His love over me, which calmed my fears and slowly
cast out all of my anxieties, one by one, while in His
presence.

My weighty insecurities started lifting off me and
were replaced by His love, which helped me become
more and more confident in who He says I am. He began revealing the special intricate details of my life that
truly make me beautiful and unique. While people may
see someone of worth now, God already saw someone
who is beautiful and wonderfully made for His plan

and glory. When I felt like something was wrong with me, God reminded me that He has a plan for me as it is written, "What no eye has seen, what no ear has heard, and what no human mind has conceived'—the things God has prepared for those that love him" (1 Corinthians 2:9). Life is exciting and full of surprises when we see how He works in our lives. May God gives us ears to hear and eyes to see Him (Proverbs 20:12).

God began showing me that there is more to life than materialism, status, superficial relationships, striving, accomplishments, and performance. His grace is so much bigger, and it covers all our weaknesses and gives us strength. And in His Word, there is life, and in His presence, there is freedom. His Word is truth, and in His Word, there is hope. He began taking over my heart, more and more, through my surrender and His sanctification. Over time, not overnight, I begin to feel alive, filled with His joy and His strength. There is no greater feeling than being in His perfect will. There is so much peace and joy that comes from being in His will. It is not always easy, but even in the storm, He is there with you, and you can face any storm because all things work out for our good (Romans 8:28).

Our culture emphasizes the importance of sex appeal. The culture wants us to believe that our beauty is tied to our sex appeal. The more skin we show and the more seductive we are, the more attention we get.

There is nothing wrong with wanting to be attractive or wanting attention. It's how we go about it. If we must dress provocatively or sexy to turn heads, we risk getting into a relationship that breeds lust, not love. Lust is temporary, but love is eternal. Not all attention is good attention, ladies. A great guy will love you for more than your physical attributes. He will notice the heart. Also, physical attraction is important, but what's more important is waiting for the right person. When the right person is there, in God's timing, it will be beautiful and worth celebrating because it's real. God would never want His daughters to compromise, so if you find yourself compromising your beliefs, your standards, or convictions, that person is not from the Lord. We first need to encounter the love of the Lord, so He can show us our value and lead us to the right husband. Then we will be able to recognize the right person for us because he will not only speak what is charming to our ears but have the ability to speak life to our spirit.

If a relationship starts with sex or lust, it will leave us with a sense of emptiness. Do not fool yourself into believing what the world teaches, that it's just sex or that a guy will not stick around if you don't have sex with him. If you're meeting men with those standards, you're shopping in the wrong departments. Reclaim your senses and conviction. God will give you something so much better. Delight yourself in the Lord, and

He will give you the desires of your heart (Psalm 37:4). When we come to Christ, we realize that God sees us differently and that we are more than our wrinkles, body size, or clothes. God looks at our hearts (1 Samuel 16:7).

Reflection questions:

- How has culture played a role in your life today?
- How has your family played a role in your up-bringing and perspective?

Identity

At one point in my life, I realized that I was unhappy, unsatisfied, and was just going through the motions of life, church, and relationships. One day, one of my friends pointed out to me that I didn't seem to be happy. I attended church, hung out with friends, but my heart was still empty, and I began fighting depression. I reached a point where I felt sad and hopeless, and I felt like there was no point in being a believer. I didn't know that God had better, bigger plans for my life at that time. I did not know that the problem was my internal narrative, where I believed that my joy would be found if I was married. And if my family were doing well, then God would have answered my prayers. But my prayers for my family were not answered, and I was not married, so why was I still a believer? Where were all the promises of God? I felt so disappointed that the enemy began to oppress me with thoughts of suicide and made me want to abandon Christ as my Lord since He did not do what I had been praying for. I began crying out to God. I began begging for Him to take my life. God heard my prayer and answered me. I felt the presence of God enter my room, and He said, "No, she will live, and she will live for my glory!" Suddenly, all of the depression symptoms lifted, and I was set free. It was such a powerful encounter with His presence that I felt a shift happen right at that moment. Afterward, I began seeking God, and He began revealing my identity to me and guiding my steps. As mentioned, in Jeremiah 29:11, "For I know the plans I have for you," declares the Lord, "plans to prosper you, and not harm you, plans to give you hope and a future." Aren't you so thankful that we serve a God that hears our prayers and answers us?

Little did I know, the plans the Lord had for me were so much greater than I ever imagined. I was only focused on getting married and believing that it was what I was missing and that marriage was where my happiness would be found, but God had so much more in store for me. Praise God that He knows how to lead us and how to make a way even in the wilderness where all seems dry and dead. Christ died so we would live and live with abundance (John 10:10, NLT). There are fountains that don't run dry in Him and a thirst within us that only He can satisfy. I didn't know about it until I began growing in Him, and He began revealing more and more of Himself to me. Suddenly, I understood why being focused on the clothes I wore, make-up, status, accomplishments, and guys never filled me. There is so much more to what we are called to as believers and as His bride.

I still remember how much time I would waste dwelling and talking about my crushes repeatedly. That singular focus became a spiritual stronghold in my life. I was surprised nobody told me that I was crazy or that I needed help because my focus on my crushes was obsessive and unhealthy. Another component to my obsession to be in a relationship was the pressure from my culture and from our society. We need to stop portraying that singleness is all about finding the right person and settling down. Our culture presents romance as this superficial Disneyland fantasy. Boy meets girl, boy pursues girl, boy wins girl, boy marries girl, and they live happily ever after. Nobody talks about what happens after the fairytale ends and how much work relationships require. Or how marriage, by God's design, is meant to represent the Trinity of God and bring Him glory. The reality is that a lot of relationships don't end happily ever after. There are struggles, there are difficult seasons, and they require a lot of work.

I believe the Lord desires to release identity over His sons and daughters! I believe that the Lord wants to pour out His love and purpose into our lives, so we can become carriers of His love, carriers of His spirit, and carriers of His truth. We are called to shine bright for

WEAR THAT CROWN, GIRL

Him (Matthew 5:16). And therefore, we need to run with all of our hearts toward the Father to be filled up with Him and His truth, so we can run and not grow weary. We need His empowerment through the Holy Spirit. We need His direction. We need His refinement. There is so much more to where the Lord has called us if we just believe and allow Him to complete the process that He began (Philippians 1:6). This process starts from a place of surrender to the Lord.

If you're not sure how to surrender to the Lord, say this simple prayer: "Lord, I come before You just as I am. Please cleanse me, refine me, and make me new. I am Your creation, and I am Your beloved. I am who You say I am, and I bind any words others have spoken against me in the name of Jesus. Reveal my identity to me. Speak Your truth, hope, and faith over me. I want to know You and Your love. I surrender my dreams, my desires, and expectations to You and instead ask that You fill me up to overflowing. Teach me and lead me by the Holy Spirit. May my eyes and ears be open to You when You speak. I pray all this in Jesus' name."

I believe that the Lord has something special to release to those who are single and not married. There is a reason for this special season in your life, and may you rejoice in it. The season will come to an end one day, but have you done all that the Lord has called you to do? You are not a mistake, and there is nothing wrong with you just because you're single. I believe that the Lord has set people aside for such a time as this, to be His vessels, to be the carriers of His love, to be ambassadors of His kingdom here on earth. And if you surrender your singleness to Him as an offering, there is so much more that He could do through you for His glory. Surrender your dreams, surrender your desires, and your expectations. Let God be God in your life, and He will fill you with life. "Whoever finds their life will lose it, and whoever loses their life for my sake will find it (Matthew 10:39). When we surrender to His perfect will, we thrive, we glow differently, and we live confidently with purpose.

We are not single because we are desperate, we are not single because we are picky, but we are single because the Lord has chosen us for this generation to be His light! There are certain things that some of us are called to before we are married. I'm not saying that if you're single, stay single forever. I'm saying that if you are putting yourself out there, praying to meet someone, and you've tried everything, but the Lord has not opened a relationship for you yet, then maybe that's not His plan yet. May you live to glorify God. May you delight in Him, just as He does in you. Because when we delight in Him, it will bring Him glory and pleasure (Psalm 37:4 GNT).

Reflection questions:
- How do you see yourself?
- How does the world see you?
- How do you want others to see you?
- Who does the Lord say you are?

Overcoming
Disappointments

While going through life and navigating through the motions of singlehood, you may begin to wonder, "Am I ever going to get married?" "It feels like I've been single forever!" "Why does it never work out?" I remember after my two younger sisters married. I was feeling like, "Does anybody see me? Or see how unfair life can seem?" You may be feeling similar to what I was feeling after witnessing your friend or family members getting married, and you may feel like it's unfair.

If you've ever felt this way, you are not alone! At some point, after dating a lot of counterfeits, you begin to wonder if your prince is ever going to come. I want to reassure you that he will come in God's perfect timing. I wish I had a more specific date for you. But most of the time, God doesn't reveal certain things to us because He knows the plans He has for us. And we need to seek Him so that He can reveal His secrets to us (Jeremiah

33:3). In the secret place, He reveals His secrets to us when we seek Him with all our heart.

We all walk through disappointment at some point in our lives. You can be disappointed because you're single or had a relationship not work out the way you planned. Disappointments are a part of life, and we all must go through them. They're not pleasant, but if allowed, they will teach a lot. How do you deal with disappointment? You could turn to substances or alcohol, as many people do. Or you could go to the Lord and release your feelings and thoughts around your disappointment. In other words, you need to feel it and grieve it. The loss is real. Embrace the Lord's love toward you and ask Him to fill you with all hope that surpasses understanding. And ask Him to fill you with the joy that only comes from Him through His strength, to be empowered by His Holy Spirit and His comfort as you continue to wait.

A lot of times, we think that God doesn't understand us or hear us. But He does! He sees your every thought and every move. You matter to Him, and He grieves when you grieve. Allow Him into that space, be vulnerable, and open to Him your desires, your dreams, your disappointments, your expectations, and afterward, release them to the Lord and surrender. And know that He is a good Father, who loves you. Another important thing to note is that, even though your desire for a mate has not been fulfilled yet, that does not correlate with the Father's love toward you. He loves you so much, and only God knows the reason why you are single, but you can trust Him no matter whatever season you are in. And if you need some hope, cry out to Him for that hope. It's okay to ask for help if you're tired of the season and you feel like you can't go on anymore. He is there right next to you, walking you through it.

If we surrender our disappointment to the Lord and our tears, He can do so much greater with them. I'm a strong believer that the Lord rewards those who seek Him and put their trust in Him. Just because your relationship did not work out the way you wanted it to does not mean that you have to give up on your dream. The Lord knows our hearts, our desires, and our dreams, and in His timing, He will fill our hearts' desires if we surrender them to Him.

I look back now over the course of my life and can't recall the many things I was disappointed over when I did not get them. There were a lot of things. And I would cry so much. s I look back and reflect, I see that the Lord was right. So many great things have happened because of those disappointments or closed doors. If it wasn't for those closed doors, the right and better doors for my life would not have been opened. Another great illustration is when you see good parents and how they discipline their kids. They do not give their children everything they want because they know what their children need now. It's the same thing with our good Father. He knows how to give good gifts to us. We can trust our Father in heaven that closed doors are blessings from Him.

Another important thing to understand is that sometimes we have to re-surrender things a few times, and we may have to undergo numerous disappointments and grieve specific relationships or pains a few times. There are layers to healing and breakthroughs. So, give yourself grace to heal, and get over the disappointment. Some people recover more quickly than others, and others take a little bit longer to get there, but it doesn't change the fact that the Lord hears our cries and will repay our patience, as we trust in Him with His goodness and kindness to us.

Reflection Question:

- Are there any areas of disappointment that you have not yet released to the Lord?

Our Timeline isn't God's Timeline
(But God's Timing is Always Perfect!)

Waiting is never easy. Waiting is not a passive act. Waiting patiently requires faith in the Lord through acts of trust. As you wait on the Lord to bring His promise into fruition or respond to your prayer, ignite your faith and trust in Him. Without faith, we cannot please God, for those that come to the Lord must first believe that He exists and that He rewards those who earnestly seek Him (Hebrews 11:6). Secondly, make steps toward your promise. This can look like starting to look after yourself, so you can look great for your future spouse. This may also look like you are open to meeting new people if that is where you feel led by the Holy Spirit. However, God is going to bring the person to you.

One time, I really liked this guy, Steve, and I was praying for the Lord to bless us. And every time I tried to pray about us, it felt like there was a wall between the Lord and me as if we weren't on the same page. It felt like that could be related to the person I wanted to end up with. The Lord gave me a vision where I saw myself trying to put my foot inside a shoe that was too small for me. And I kept trying to force this foot to go inside this shoe that wasn't my size. In the beginning, I ignored the feeling that something just did not feel right with Steve. Over time, however, it became very apparent that we were two different people who did not belong together. We had different beliefs about God and different values.

I think a lot of us do this at times when we try to settle or compromise with the Lord. We are like, "Why is this shoe not fitting me? I like this shoe, and I don't want to give it up," and the Lord is trying to say, "This is not your shoe size." The Lord knows what's best for us, and we can trust Him. One of the best ways to live is to surrender everything at His feet and watch Him work in our lives to bring out the best in us. His ways are so much higher than our ways, and His thoughts are also higher than our thoughts, so what makes us think that we are wiser than He? His plans for us are so much bigger than we are. And He knows where we're going to end up, so He knows what shoe size we need. We make decisions based on what we see, but God knows our past, present, and our future.

Some of us just need to give up the expectations that we have or the timelines that we have placed upon ourselves or others. These expectations or timelines may not be the Lord's timeline or His will. And if we don't give them up, we might become more disappointed and miss what the Lord intends for us. I can recall one of my friends at church met this guy named Joe when we went out to eat someplace after service one day. She became interested in Joe. However, Joe didn't ask her out, but Samuel (who became her husband) did. At first, she hesitated because Samuel was not physically her type, but the connection that was made that night was evident. A few weeks later, she mentioned that she was going out with Samuel because she took it in prayer to the Lord. The Lord revealed to her that Samuel was the real deal and what she had been praying for. Ever since that first date, they have been inseparable and have been happily married for five years.

Another thing that makes waiting hard is when you feel the pressure to be married because of your age. This is especially true if your girlfriends are getting married, or others are getting married for the second time around, and you're still waiting your turn. It can even seem as if God has passed you by. The enemy likes to use the idea of what we don't have to make us start complaining, throwing a pity party, or start doubting God that our turn is coming. But I want to remind you that you are not forgotten or unseen. The Lord's timeline is not our timeline, and if you're waiting, be prepared to receive more.

When we look in the Word of God, a good example of people of faith is Abraham and Sarah. God calls them people of faith. God formed a covenant with them that they were going to be parents of a big group of people, and Sarah would have a son who was going to start this blessing off. Abraham and Sarah believed God's promise, but the only limitation that Abraham and Sarah faced was that they were becoming old. When we read about Abraham and Sarah, we see how the Lord said that Abraham and Sarah would have a child born to them. At first, I'm sure they were excited about the word that they received and filled with gratitude and anticipation. But time went on, and then they were in their fifties, sixties, eighties, and nineties. You have to imagine that from time to time, they thought, "Is God's promise still going to happen that we are going to have a baby? Maybe God changed His mind? Maybe I misunderstood the promise."

I'm sure that at that moment, they felt like their days of conceiving a child were overdue to their age. Anybody feel me on that? It can be the same thing in our lives— sometimes we must wait for a very, very, very long time for a promise to come true. And during those pivotal moments in our lives is when God uses that season to shape our faith the greatest. Faith wouldn't be called faith without the process of waiting and going through the impossible. If it was possible, then how could God get the glory? Genuine faith has to go through testing to reveal its purity. So, if you're in the waiting process, have faith and rest in the promise by allowing the Lord to do the inner work that needs to be done in your life. I know it's not easy, and I know it doesn't feel pleasant sometimes. But the rewards are going to be priceless and the fruit extravagant. Faith without works is dead (James 2:17). If you persist, you will have the fruit to show for your faith.

Because we live in the natural world, it's sometimes difficult to see things from God's perspective. But God is more focused on our inner work than the outer man. During my most difficult moments of life, I always cried out to God for Him to show me from His perspective how He sees me and what He was teaching me in the moment. That way, it was so much easier to surrender my timeline because I was reminded how big my God is, how full of wisdom, and that His ways are always higher, better, and sovereign. Another amazing thing that happens when we pray to see our situation from God's perspective is the earthly desires start falling away. We realize that true riches are inside of us, like His word, His glory, His joy, His peace, His hope, and eternal things that can never be taken away.

> **Prayer:** *"Father God, I come to You right now. I release to You any expectations or any timelines that I created or am holding onto. I ask for You to instead fill me with Your plan, Your dreams, Your passions, Your desires, and Your fire. Help me to see things from Your perspective, Father. Help me to understand Your ways for my life right now. Even when things don't make sense, help me to hang onto Your hope and Your promises. In Jesus' name, I pray."*

Reflection Question:

- Are there any expectations or timelines that need to be surrendered to the Lord?

If Your Waiting is Long, Be Prepared for Extra

Once upon a time, there was a lady who thought she knew what was best for her, so she held onto her ideas of how life should be instead of what God thought it should be. When we have an expectancy for the Lord to show up, it leaves room for unexpected miracles, wonders, and surprises from the Lord: in other words, to live in the fullness of Christ. Living in the fullness of Christ means living full lives in every area of our lives: spiritually, mentally, and physically. My question to you is, "Who is on the throne of your life decisions?" When we have something in our life that did not turn out the way we expected it to, we can trust that the Lord is a good Father and that He knows what He's doing. Even when in the natural realm, it seems as if nothing is happening or logically doesn't make sense, you can be assured God is at work.

Also, I believe that the Lord is saying because of your waiting, be prepared to be blown away. The longer the wait, the greater the reward. If you're in the waiting season, whether waiting for a relationship, a job, or a promise, then be expectant that the Lord is never late, but He always shows up at the right time. He remains faithful even if we give up on Him (2 Timothy 2:13).

Do you not know?
Have you not heard?
The Lord is the everlasting God,
the Creator of the ends of the earth.
He will not grow tired or weary,
and His understanding no one can fathom.
He gives strength to the weary
and increases the power of the weak.
Even youths grow tired and weary,
and young men stumble and fall;
but those who hope in the Lord
will renew their strength.
They will soar on wings like eagles;
they will run and not grow weary,
they will walk and not be faint
Isaiah 40:28-31

May you be strengthened by *the power of His Spirit* as you wait! He is who He says He is! There is no victory without a fight, and we don't know how strong we are until we go through the fire. A heart that's gone through the waiting period undergoes a testing of faith. You can't be trusted until you've been tested. You can't say you're faithful if you have never been tempted. But when you come out on the other side of the waiting period, be prepared to receive so much more. It's going to be worth it!

In Romans, chapter eight talks about how when we are waiting on the Lord, then the waiting is enlarging us on the inside.

> That is why waiting does not diminish us, any more than waiting diminishes a pregnant mother. We are enlarged in the waiting. We, of course, don't see what is enlarging us. But the longer we wait, the larger we become, and the more joyful our expectancy. Meanwhile, the moment we get tired in the waiting, God's Spirit is right alongside helping us along. If we don't know how or what to pray, it doesn't matter. He does our praying in and for us, making prayer out of our wordless signs, our aching groans. He knows us far better than we know ourselves, knows our pregnant

condition, and keeps us present before God. That's why we can be so sure that every detail in our lives of love for God is worked into something good.

Romans 8:25-28 (MSG)

Be in good cheer if you are waiting on the Lord. The Lord rewards those who wait upon Him, who put their trust in him. In the Bible, there are a lot of great examples of those who waited and how, after the promise was fulfilled, it was bigger than anything they imagined. For example, let's look at the life of Joseph (Genesis 37). He was given a dream of how his entire family would bow down to him, and his brothers hated him because of it. But after the dream, his brothers sold Joseph into slavery. Afterward, Joseph became in charge at the king's palace. Eventually, there was a famine in the country where they lived and nearby, so everyone eventually came down to Joseph for help because of the famine, including his own family. As we continue reading Joseph's story, we notice that he becomes so blessed that he has status, money, and provision. And afterward, he gets reconnected with his family, who end up coming to him for help, kneeling before him. I believe that Joseph's promise was fulfilled after witnessing the Lord's glory through his story. I bet the Lord worked on Joseph's heart throughout his life before the promise was fulfilled, and when it was fulfilled, there must have been so much overwhelming joy.

You can wait with hope, or you can wait hopeless! When you're waiting with hope, even if you're single, you're not going to be desperate enough to just go along with just any available person who shows interest. You are waiting for the right one for you. That's God's best for you! You will know who the best one is for you because you will have peace, and you will have confirmation. The Bible says, "The blessing of the Lord makes you happy, and there is no sorrow in it" (Proverbs 10:22, AMP).

Why Relationships and Community Matter

In your season of singleness, take the time to pour into your existing relationships. And if you don't have any friendships, this is the season to develop friendships, so you can learn how to be a good friend to God, others, and yourself. Be a good steward with your relationships (family and friendships). Friendships teach us a lot of relational things about ourselves and others. In your relationships, you get to know who you are, how you respond, how to be vulnerable, what bothers you, and how to deal with conflict. And trust me, this is also a preparation for marriage or a dating relationship. If we are not careful with our words or our actions towards others and if we caused injury to others, then we may not be ready yet to be in a serious relationship. In the process of working through our relationships, the Lord will point out certain things in our lives that are in our hearts that may need pruning or healing. Allow the Lord to teach you how to do relationships in a healthy way and how that looks like while you are in a single season. We all have different areas that we need to work on. It's not about perfection but about stewarding relationships and understanding how to value ourselves and others through the process.

Singleness season is also a time to learn how to have those difficult conversations that we don't usually like to have but need to have. We need to learn how to navigate certain conversations with love, truth, gentleness, and humility. A lot of the time, we think that God is only concerned about our spiritual growth, and we compartmentalize God, but He is just as concerned about how we treat others. God is bigger than our boxes or our perceptions of Him. He is involved in every detail of our lives, including our relationships, our hearts, our finances, our character, and how we treat others. Relationships will help you understand how to relate to others and how to connect with others and do life together. There are so many blessings in a family where love, unity, and humility reign. It brings God glory here on earth and in heaven because where there is a strong family, there is a strong foundation for their children, their grandchildren, and future generations.

Sometimes, when we live in community with others, we can lose track of focus during that season of cultivating a relationship with our Lord. We do this by giving our primary focus toward dating and whom we are crushing on. There is certainly nothing wrong with talking about whether we are dating or sharing information about our love life, but when that's the centerpiece of all of our conversations, it overtakes God's place in our hearts. And that's where I was. I remember all my friends that I met in my single days. My girlfriends and I would always be talking and updating others on our love lives as if there was nothing else for us to talk about. God was like this beautiful idea or accessory that I would put on and wear on Sundays. I would go on Sundays to church, fulfill my ministry duties, get a check mark for the day, and that was it.

God wants our whole heart because He is a jealous God. It's not because He's bad or greedy, but because His love for us is so strong. He doesn't want anything to take first place before Him. We can love somebody, and we can also love God at the same time, so our heart is divided. If our heart is divided, then God cannot reign fully in our hearts or in our lives. When our hearts are saturated with God's fire and love, our passion and affections are directed towards our Father. We want to please Him, so, therefore, we live fully for His purpose and for His glory. It is easier to live fully for God in our singleness than if we are married. Paul talks about it in the Bible in 1 Corinthians. Once we are married, we have to think about our significant other, so our interest is divided. I believe there's so much greatness to the singleness season. It is not mentioned enough in the church or in our communities about the blessings, rewards, and their impact on our lives and in God's kingdom. Singleness season is special and significant because it can bear so much fruit for God's kingdom as we pursue Him above all, experiencing this intimacy with the Father.

Another reason why it's important to surround ourselves in community is that it gives us perspective about ourselves, others, and the world around us. It makes us feel as if we are not alone. All individuals have difficult moments, and we can relate to each other in some capacity. For example, my good friends that I have known for more than ten years eventually got married, and in the beginning, it was fun, great, and easy for them to be married. But over the course of time, they had kids, changed jobs, and started experiencing issues at home with their marriages. At some point, my friend was considering if a divorce would be a better solution than to go through the struggle. She even told me that she wished that she was single like me. Witnessing my friends going through these seasons in their lives made me realize that no matter if you are married or single, you are going to have to go through difficulties, and the grass will seem greener on the other side. It's not. We all have different seasons that we will have to walk through, but we can take heart in the Lord who created us to be overcomers. And we can find peace and comfort in Him.

Over the past fifteen years, a few close friends and family got married and have been married for quite a while. And after talking to them about their marriages, some of them wish they had stayed single a little bit longer because marriage also has its ups and downs, and it doesn't solve our issues. I don't know if you have people in your lives that you could reach out to, whether your mentors or somebody else that you trust to ask what marriage is really like. I guarantee you if they are honest with you and you see how married life is at their home, you'll realize that it's not always happy moments, which will put things into perspective for you.

Another reason why it's important to be in the community is to find couples who have been married for a long time and have a good marriage, so you could learn from them. Surround yourself with healthy role models in your life that can model a healthy marriage for you or how to do life on life together.

Reflection Questions:

- Do you agree that community matters in our lives?
- What positive experiences have you or others experienced personally?
- What negative experiences have you witnessed?

Navigating Rejections

We all experience rejection at some point. Most of our potential interests or dating partners are not going to end up marrying us. So, take a breath if that needs to sink in because sometimes, the people around us in our lives can create this false expectation that if we are dating, then we must end up getting married, which can create confusion and place unnecessary stress on couples if things do not turn out the way we wanted them. This false expectation can lead to heartbreak and the belief that we did something wrong, or else they would have stayed, or we would still be together. But I want to remind you that a rejection is a redirection (not sure who came up with this quote). Time will tell why the relationship never worked out. I believe that God has something better for us when we are rejected and gives us something better in exchange. We can find comfort when we are going through heartbreak because Scripture tells us, "The Lord is close to the broken hearted." And, He hears our cries. He sees our hearts, and He will make it right. Maybe not right away, but it will happen in due time.

One day you will be with that person who loves you the way you need to be loved, and it will be so much better than you have ever imagined. It's important to remember during those difficult moments of singleness that there is nothing wrong with you. Sometimes, people are just not compatible, or it's not God's plan for our lives to be in relationship with a certain person. If you can learn to see it that way instead of taking it personally, then it will be so much easier for you to get through it. Someone's behavior towards you may have nothing to do with you at all. Most of the time, we think that others treat us because we have done something wrong, but most of the time, it's just where they are in life. I heard someone describe themselves as low-hanging fruit (not worth much) because they have slept with others. Just because you sleep with someone does not mean you are less worthy. That is a lie from the enemy. I want to remind you that in God's eyes, there is no such thing as low-hanging fruit. You may have some history, and if you surrender it to God, watch Him use that for your good. In God's eyes, we are all His children, and He has no favorite.

The Lord is not about rejection. Quite the opposite. His heart is for you, and He wants to bless you. So, if you are ever in God's presence, there is only love, hope, and faith. The enemy, on the other hand, lies and tries to bring us down, so tell him to leave by standing on the Word of God. If you have gone through a situation or relationship where you felt rejection, I pray for healing right now over you and complete wholeness over you. I hope you come to realize that it was God's protection for you if a relationship did not work out. A lot of the time, we get so attached to the idea of a person or relationship, without knowing if that person is what we need. We think we know our crush, but the Lord's ways and thoughts are higher than ours. He knows what's best for us. Trust that He is a good Father, trust in His goodness, and in who He says He is in His Word. And remember, the Lord is so pleased ravaged by you. He delights in you. And He is going to give you something better. One day you'll look back and realize how grateful you are that relationship that made you feel rejected never worked out.

Have you been in a bad relationship or on a bad date? It might have been with somebody who was not even a believer. If you have, then when you meet the person who you are meant to be with, you will realize how different it is. It is so different when the Lord is in it. You will not be confused or hesitant about if they're the right person for you. While you are in your single season, keep praying for your spouse and that the Lord prepares both of you, bringing you together in His timing, so that you may be a blessing to each other and for your future generations.

There were a few moments in my life when I was interested in somebody, but I did not have any peace. And it's not that they did anything wrong, but it came from inside of me. Then the more I would talk about that person or think about them, the more my anxiety would increase. Finally, after I would completely let go of the possibility of even going out with the person, that's when my peace would come back. I always thought that it was so crazy. After this happened a few more times, I began to understand that it was God speaking to me that they were not mine. A few people would start to tell me that I was picky or maybe I was fighting anxiety because I would not date the men who were interested in me. It would really bring me into a state of confusion until I realized that it was not the Lord speaking to me. As time went by, I began to understand and realize that the Lord was protecting me from the individuals who weren't meant for me. Although, in those moments of letting go of the crushes, I would get sad and not understand God's ways. I remembered that the waiting would be so worth it once it was over, and it would reveal why relationships have not worked out with anyone else. The Lord told me in my season of singleness that I would praise Him when I did get together with my husband, it takes humility and complete trust in the Lord in the waiting, but we will not be disappointed.

I think we all have experienced moments where we just want to give up on God or on our love life and just date whomever. Sometimes, we even date others because we are lonely or afraid of being alone. But I want to challenge you to get more serious about your walk. Ask the Lord to fill those needs that we have for a companion with His love and to help you get them met in healthy ways. This may look like you are going on dates with Him, or road trips with Him, to simply delight in Him. Because the Word of God says that those who delight themselves in Him, He gives them the desires of their heart (Psalm 37). Additionally, pray for God to fill your heart with so much love and whatever else you need, so you are not falling for another person for the wrong reasons. We all have needs, and it's important to identify them and see how we can get them met in healthy ways. For example, if it's a need for intimacy, then it can be filled by close friends.

Reflection Question:
- How do you handle rejection?

God-Confidence Versus Self-Confidence

When our confidence is aligned with the Lord, then we are confident because of who we are in Him. Through knowing our identity in Christ, we are naturally filled with confidence. However, when our confidence is tied with the things we have, like money, status, looks, physical attributes, or whatever else, then we do not know our identity. Identity is not defined by external things. Consequently, our value has meaning because we were bought at a high price when Jesus died on the cross for you and me. That is why it's important to have our foundation built on Christ. Because when our foundation is built on the Word of God, and our identity is found in Christ, we will not be shaken because we know nothing can separate us from the love of Christ, no matter what comes our way. Not death, no illness, no mistake or guilt or shame. It is through God's revelation of His love toward us that brings down the lies and casts out fear because we know Him, and He is love. After we experience or encounter His love, we are forever changed. We know what real love looks like because He first loved us. Since God created you, He wanted you.

I've witnessed or heard this question asked all the time, "How do you respond or feel when others ask you about your singleness?" So many singles feel upset or angry when they are asked this question, so it brings me to my next point. Be confident in who God called you to be. Stay true to yourself. Anyone can get married; it's not that difficult. But, if you are waiting because you have not met the right guy or because you are waiting on the promise of God, then be confident with your status.

However, if you are insecure due to being single, you will come off insecure. How you view yourself is how others will view you. So, work on yourself. If you do not feel like you know where you are going, ask God to reveal His plans and vision for you. Also, you can ask yourself, "What am I bringing to the table?" to gain confidence. This way, you feel good about yourself and know what you are looking for. Our confidence increases when we know who we are and where we are heading. Some people are single because they can't find anyone, and others are single because they haven't found the one who is theirs. God's plans are good. Do you believe Him? If not, get with God and pour out your heart to Him and allow Him to fill you up with His love toward you.

The Word of God says that those who trust in the Lord are blessed. Cursed is the man who puts his trust in humans. Sometimes, we meet a person we really like and are attracted to, and we believe the lie that only they can bring us happiness. We put them on a pedestal in our lives and in our hearts. But the Lord wants us to be confident in Him, to boast in Him alone.

Reflection Question:

- What is your confidence in? What brings you happiness?

Each Road Has a Plan to Bring Him Glory in the End

I still remember that moment when I was praying to the Lord, asking Him why nothing ever worked out with any of the guys I dated. I remember the Lord showing me a picture of me trying to put my foot into a shoe that was too small for my foot. My foot size was bigger than the shoe, so obviously, it didn't fit. I believe the Lord was showing to me that the men that I was interested in were not the right fit for me. Although they were good men, they were not my match. So, I had to remind myself that the Lord had somebody bigger and better for me. Sometimes, the Lord prevents us from getting into relationships because He doesn't want us to settle. I can't even count the numerous times where I wanted to settle. I was tired of always being told that I was too picky, or that something must be wrong with me, etc. However, I learned that the problem was that I needed to hang onto my faith, not settle for less than God's best, and not doubt myself or God. Looking back on my crushes or the men I dated, I am so grateful that the Lord didn't allow any of them to happen.

After the shoe revelation, I became much more confident and bold because I believed the Lord's plans for me and would not change them. My years have been filled with so much restoration, healing, surprises, miracles, and blessings. I received opportunities to lead different ladies' groups, do ministry, volunteer, meet so many amazing people who have taught me so much, and have grown in intimacy with Him. He could have done all this with me being married, but it would look completely different. Praise God.

I look back now and see all these amazing fruits from being obedient to the Lord, and it pleases Him because it brought Him glory. It's an amazing experience to be used by God. He is so pleased when we are obedient and surrender all to Him, serving Him wholeheartedly. It brings Him glory. If I had gotten into the relationships that I wanted to be in, I think that my life would've turned out much differently, and I don't think I would have been able to go after the things I've done with my whole heart. Sometimes God wants us to serve Him with our singleness, and sometimes the Lord allows us to serve with somebody else. He is Lord over everyone, so allow Him to lead you and direct your steps.

Reflection Question:

- How has the Lord been leading you differently in comparison with others' lives?

Self-Acceptance

How many of us have had this experience with ourselves: we wake up, look in the mirror, and dislike what we see? Next, we identify each attribute that is unattractive, and we wish we looked like our friend or the person who is in the magazines.

It's especially difficult if we got teased for our looks or attributes by others, leaving big holes in our hearts. But God is the Creator, and He has a good reason for our imperfections. Some of us can become so fixated on the imperfections that we lose sight of what is more important: Every person God created is beautiful and good.

I reflect back on my life and the time when my sisters and I were young and would think that I was bossy. Well, as I have gotten older and wiser, a friend of mine told me that meant I was a leader. After hearing her reframe my personality trait, it stuck with me. I began thinking, *That's right, I'm a leader, so that's why I like to lead and have a vision that I would like to execute.* Of course, I had to learn to take feedback and learn how to use the "bossiness" gift in the right way for God's glory, so others did not feel like I was ordering them around. Instead, I communicated that I had a plan and needed others' help with executing it. I began watching my tone and the way I approached others, so they would understand my heart was for God's glory, and I wanted to do it in love.

Similarly, I had other things that I did not like about myself, such as being funny at times. But as I began to wonder how this trait served God's purpose in my life, I realized that it helped me and continues to help me work better with others. When people look at the way I talk or think, they can see that I do not take myself too seriously and that it's okay to be themselves around me. It helps bring down other peoples' walls and allows them to enjoy themselves. Another thing that has been a blessing is that I looked and sounded very young in my twenties and thirties. I would get upset, especially when others would forget my age, or would point it out, until a pastor of mine said to me, "It's a good thing because it probably helps the adolescents and young people you work with feel comfortable to open up around you because they think you are not that much older than them." I was shocked. I felt like I had a revelation that I never understood before. Ever since then, I have never complained about my age or my youthful appearance.

We are going to do a quick test. Ask yourself, "How do I see myself?" Take a moment and answer that question.

The reason I asked this question is for your self-awareness. If you quickly answered those questions without hesitation, then you probably have a good awareness of who you are and how you relate to others.

Next, ask yourself, "Do I accept myself?" Sometimes we are better at accepting others' flaws around us than we are at accepting our own flaws.

When we are accepting of ourselves, we are readier to meet the right person for us because we can look at them through the eyes of grace. But to accept our future spouse, we need to know ourselves. Take some time to get to know yourself by spending time dating yourself. Ask the Lord to show you where He's leading you and your future. Ask Him to dream with you, and invite Him in to show you the future, so you can get excited about the plans He has for you and your future family. It's always more powerful when individuals come together who know their identity and who can be a blessing to one another, other than coming together to draw their identities from the other person to fill those empty spaces. A lot of times, when people don't know their identity, they tend to become more codependent on others. They tend to become enmeshed in picking up others' habits, interests, and passions instead of ex-

ploring their unique individuality. It's normal to naturally adopt certain habits from people that we surround
ourselves with, but it's unhealthy when you don't know
yourself and who you are, so you lose yourself.

With the person who is meant for you, you will not
have to try to fit into his definition of who you should
be. If you find yourself changing for another person (in
a negative sense), know that this is not from the Lord.
The Lord is Spirit, where the Spirit of the Lord is, there
is freedom (2 Corinthians 3:17). There is freedom to be
yourself, there are love and acceptance, and you can see
people through the eyes of love. We all have different
areas of growth, but there's also a level of grace that
needs to be extended. There is a difference between
people close to us pointing something out to shed light
on our actions because it hurts them or us and people
criticizing from a spirit of control or manipulation. We
must know the difference.

I get it, accepting our self is not easy. But if we can
learn to surrender that weakness or part of ourselves
that we consider "ugly" or "unattractive," then the Lord
can do so much with it. God can use anything or anyone
and turn it into a miracle. He can also do so much with
a surrendered heart. Give Him those broken pieces,
and He will use them for His glory. A great example of
that is Moses. He was called to lead the Israelites out of
Egypt (talk about a calling), and His response to God

was, "Who am I, and why would the Egyptians or Israelites listen to me?" He thought that he couldn't even
speak. He looked at himself as if he was not eloquent
enough since he had a stuttering problem. And do you
know what God told him? He told him in Exodus 4:11,
"The Lord said to him, 'Who gave human beings their
mouths? Who makes them deaf or mute? Who gives
them sight or makes them blind? Is it not I, the Lord?'"

So, whenever we don't like something about ourselves, we should say, "God, you created me this way, so
I surrender it to you and not just parts that I don't like
or accept but have all of me for Your glory." God is the
potter, and we are the clay (Jeremiah 18), so we have a
part in God's plan. Only He knows who He created us
to be, so why not ask Him to reveal who you are? The
Father delights in His creation, and all that He created,
He called it good. This includes you and me.

You might be thinking, *But how can God still love me
after all that I did in the past? You don't know my past.* I may
not know your personal sins, but I know the author of
redemption. He has a good plan for you, to give you life,
to give you hope, to give you a reason to live. He wants
all of you, the beautiful parts, the not-so-beautiful
parts, and the broken pieces. He wants to heal you, He
wants to see you blossom, He wants you to be happy.
He wants you to encounter His true love and truth, so
you can be set free.

Going back to the story of Moses, he was a murderer. He had a bad temper. He killed a person. Once others found out about his sin, he ran away from Egypt. But he couldn't run away from God, and neither can we. We can easily run away from people but not from God. God can use anyone, and He will, with those who are willing and obedient. Where there is lack, He will take care of the rest. Aren't you excited for God to show up in your life?

Reflection Questions:
- Do you struggle in any areas of self-acceptance?
- What lies have you believed about yourself?
- What versus or truths can replace those lies?

Dealing with Shame & Guilt

On July 15th, 2015, I moved into my own place for the first time. It was one of the best experiences of my life. I could decorate my place the way I wanted. I could even walk around naked if I wanted. I could watch TV, cook, and do whatever I wanted to, and nobody would have to know about it. To sum it up, I felt like I was in heaven for the first year after moving out on my own. It was such a shift from what I was used to because I had always lived with someone. However, eventually, the honeymoon phase ended, and I began to feel lonely.

And that's when I really began desiring a relationship the most. So, I took matters into my own hands by getting out there to find a guy. I knew that the Lord had a plan for my love life, but I was tired of waiting, tired of praying, tired of believing. At one point, I even thought God's plan was ridiculous and decided instead to find a guy through some dating apps. I began talking to a few of the guys, and most of them were unbelievers. I tried to meet a believer but came to realize that even the ones who said they were believers were not really committed to their faith. So, the dating pool was just more of a hookup place for most of the people on there than about actually getting to genuinely know someone. However, I was determined to be in a relationship, so I pushed myself for about a month. Long story short, I didn't meet anyone that was compatible. Afterward, I realized how I was getting carried away with the apps and began to feel like there was something unhealthy taking place in my life because I was becoming obsessive and felt darkness over the experience. The guys on the apps were not from the Lord, and I knew that I needed to stop this before the situation escalated and got out of control to the point where I would be unrecognizable to myself and others. I knew it was wrong for me to be on those apps, to begin with, because the Lord told me specifically to close those dating sites since I would not be meeting my future husband there. I ended up talking to men who I met at the dating sites and doing things that were so out of character for me that I regretted.

After about a month, I woke up on a Sunday morning and had this revelation that the whole situation felt dark and that if I continued the path I was on, I would lose my purity and the person who I once was due to God's grace and protection. Suddenly, I was overcome with conviction and so much love from the Father to come back to Him that it overshadowed my whole place, and I felt like there was a room full of angels and God rejoicing in my living room. I was overcome with so much joy that I had never felt before and began worshipping God. Then I heard the Lord say, "I'm not giving you over to just anyone" and "Feed my sheep." I went to church that day, and during worship, I saw Jesus washing my feet, and I also saw the cross with Jesus on it and felt His love for all. His love was so massive and huge enough to love everyone on this planet. It was a powerful encounter.

Afterward, I realized that nothing that I did made Jesus love me less and that all my guilt or shame has no business in God's presence because I repented and was made new. But we have an enemy, and he wants God's children to doubt God's Word and promises over their lives. He loves to use guilt and shame toward God's children to keep them from getting close to God and living with life full of joy, freedom, peace, and hope. We can also see how that enemy works since creation started when we read about "The Fall" in the book of Genesis, chapter 3: "Now the serpent was craftier than any of the wild animals the Lord God had made. He said to the woman, Did God really say, 'You must not eat from any tree in the garden?'"

When a seed is planted, which is the Word of God, the enemy's first goal is to what? To plant doubt in your mind. If he accomplishes this, then he has an in with us. So, he starts speaking to us if we are listening. However, we need to cut him off completely, as written in James 4:7, "Submit yourselves, then, to God. Resist the devil, and he will flee from you." After God told me to get off those dating sites, I should have done it right away, but the enemy tried to tempt me to stay on, just to see what happened, so I did. I remembered the shame that followed me after those interactions with the few guys that I met and did things that I should not have done. I realized that guilt or shame brings us down, making us feel unworthy of love, but I want to remind you today that you are worthy, you are valuable, and your past doesn't have to define who you are today. Each day is a fresh new start to get back up again and try again. Keep crying out to God for help to get you out of the hole. He gives strength to the weak and power to the weary (Isaiah 40:29).

The enemy is always prowling around trying to seduce us into sin. He tries to learn our weaknesses and how we think so he can get us sidetracked from fulfilling God's plan for our lives. He especially looks for the moments when we are weak or have our guard down, so he can move in. He does this in a couple of ways. One of the ways is by planting doubt in our minds. Has there ever been a moment in your life where suddenly, you start getting guilty or ashamed of yourself? Who planted that in your mind?

The enemy tries to deceive us into believing lies. If he knows that you're not strong in the area of your identity through Christ, then guess what? He is going to use guilt, shame, or condemnation against you. However, the Word of God is stronger than anything in this world, including the devil. The Word says, "Submit yourselves, then, to God. Resist the devil, and he will flee from you" (James 4:7). This means that you confidently and boldly stand up to him directly on the premise of the Word of God and faith. You need to declare that you are righteous by the blood of Jesus. And that through Jesus Christ, your sins are wiped away. You are a new creation through Christ.

Another tactic the enemy uses is through identifying our temptations and putting them in front of us. For example, if you have a weakness for money (money is not bad unless it becomes an idol for us), then he's going to use money to gain access into your heart. And his goal is to make sure that the Lord is not the Lord in your heart. He would rather it be money, materialism, busyness, or anything else. If he has succeeded in swaying you away from God, then he knows that you are a bait for him.

However, you have a helper and an intercessor named Jesus, so run to the Father, worship Him in the presence where His glory dwells. Turn on worship music, meet with Him face-to-face. Speak to Him heart-to-heart. He will listen when we seek Him with all our heart. And get into His Word, so He can cleanse your spirit. If you do these two things, no matter what the enemy tries to seduce you with or tempt you with, you will succeed and be victorious in the name of Jesus Christ! Declare your victory through Christ, and watch, the devil will flee.

Reflection Questions:
- Are there any areas that you have feelings of shame or guilt?
- Who can you speak/confess to who is a safe person in your life to help you forgive yourself?

Do Not Settle

A young lady came into my office for counseling. I will call her Sabrina in this book to protect her identity. Sabrina was slender, good-looking, and is still young. She was maybe in her 30s. She described a relationship that she had been in for about seven years. Sabrina explained that her boyfriend did not take her out, almost at all. He did not engage in any activities with her, he did not like being around her family, and he did not want to talk about or go in for counseling to improve their relationship. She continued and explained that it was partly since he had medical issues and that they limited him in a lot of things. But she said it's okay because Sabrina also had some medical issues as well. The reason she came to my office was that she thought that they would have been married by then, but he did not want to get married. She didn't know what to do because she felt that she couldn't live without him, and if she did break up with him, then nobody would want her. Sounds familiar, doesn't it?

Am I picky, or am I settling? Those are hard questions sometimes to understand. You know you are settling when you are not entirely happy with someone. When you are with the one who is meant for you, they should make you smile by just being next to you. The right one is someone who understands you and who has similar beliefs and values, who does not make you compromise in any way. It does not mean they have everything on your list for a mate, but they do need to have the important ones. Sometimes, we see others, and they marry for the wrong reasons, such as for money, status, or just physical beauty. But you want to marry your best friend, who you know for sure is yours.

We don't have to go overboard with our list for our future spouse, but a list gives us a starting place, so we can know what we think we want. And if someone (who is interested in us) may not have everything on our list then, be open because what we need might look different than what's on that list. Being picky is when we nitpick things that are not a big deal. Like not liking the way a person eats at the table. Remember, nobody is perfect in every way. On the flip side, we do not want to settle either. The best way to navigate a relationship is to keep in mind your values, beliefs, and actions that severely impact your future while praying to God to direct your steps.

When we settle, we marry the wrong person due to ignoring the signs that they are not right for us, and later we may end up divorcing them. I have witnessed so many marriages fall apart due to certain unhealthy behaviors that start to surface after marriage, such as drinking, immorality, lying, partying, cheating, pornography addictions, and many other addictions as well. Just because people go to church does not mean that they are believers.

I remember how I met up with a friend one time, and she told me her coworker asked her out on a date, and she accepted. However, during the date, the guy asked her about how she felt about sex before marriage. The guy was appalled that she believed that the Bible says that sex before marriage is a sin. His interpretation was that sex before marriage was okay as long as they were in a committed relationship. Now, I'm sure there are others out there who believe the same way my friend's date did, and this just goes to show how different our beliefs and convictions are. In this example, if my friend had stayed with him, then she would have been settling for less than God's best.

One time, I worked as a manager at a day program. My boss, who was also the owner, began to show interest in me. I came to like him as well over time, even though he was not a believer. I prayed a lot about him because I really liked him but wanted the Lord's blessing on it. One night, I was on bent knees in prayer before the Lord because I was in agony over this guy. I wanted to be with the guy but felt torn because he was not a believer, and God did not bless the relationship. As I cried out to God, suddenly the Lord's presence filled my room, and He began speaking to me. He showed me how broken I was because of my relationship with my father and how I desired male attention and love because of my lack of it growing up. He also revealed to me His real, soft, and unconditional love for me. He said that "I know you feel torn between choosing the guy or Me, but just know that, no matter what, Anna, I will always love you." Those words wreaked me, and I started sobbing. I could feel this tangible love for me that began healing those spaces in my heart that needed it. Also, in the midst of that encounter, the Holy Spirit begins showing me that if I did date the guy, I would get pregnant out of wedlock and eventually leave him because I would have realized that I wanted to be with a believer eventually and return back to Church. What a powerful encounter and revelation that was for me, that I was able to not make a mistake by settling with that guy.

I had a few other dates, where I knew that if I stayed with him, then I would be settling. One night, after I came home from a date, I realized how much better life is with the Lord. The guy I dated was a good guy; however, we were not equally yoked. I was praying through the entire time we began talking, and the Lord gave me His answer right away by removing any excitement or interest. When you don't feel the Lord in it, that's when you know that a person isn't for you. There are a lot of counterfeits, but the one who is from the Lord, you will know in your heart.

God taught me that the one for you will be someone who adds to your life, not subtracts. Relationships are not supposed to feel like a burden or an assignment. In Scripture, the Lord showed me that a man who is yours will evoke your beauty. In other words, he brings out the best in you.

Sometimes the chemistry with a person can be so wonderful and so great, yet miss the most important thing, which is the Lord. I know that some people would try to talk me into giving the guys a second chance and say, "Well, you can always pray that he comes to the Lord; maybe that's the Lord's will for your life." Thank God, I know my identity, and I know it's not to get married to a man that I must lead to the Lord, who would have wanted me to compromise a few things in the dating phase. Compromise is not from the Lord!

The Lord is extravagant in His love and mercy. He wouldn't give us someone who is not a full blessing from Him. Daughters of God, the Bible says that there is no grievance with the blessing of the Lord (Proverbs

10:22). Clearly, how can my heart not grieve if someone doesn't love the Lord? And how can two walk together unless they agree? Confusion is not from the Lord, either. Let's not settle for crumbs; I believe the Lord has better things in store for you.

I noticed that those who don't know where their identity is in Christ settle for crumbs. I want to remind you that you are beautiful, fearfully, and wonderfully made in the image of God. The Lord loves you so much. You don't have to settle for crumbs. There's so much more in store for you; invite Him into your heart and allow Him to pour out His love upon you. Then you'll understand how much worth you carry because of who your Father is.

Here are a few questions you can ask yourself that might be helpful to determine if you're settling:

1. Does he bring out the best in you?
2. Does he support you? In your dreams and your calling, in your vision?
3. Are you proud of him?
4. Could you love him and commit to him for the rest of your life? And not have any regrets?
5. Has he gotten to know the real you and love you for you? Without trying to change you?

The person that's meant for us will be somebody who brings out the best in us. When we read the verse below, sometimes I think it only applies to the people who are married. However, it also communicates Jesus and His bride, which translates to His love for us as well personally.

> Husbands go all out in your love for your wives, exactly as Christ did for the church—a love marked by giving, not getting. Christ's love makes the church whole. His words evoke her beauty. Everything he does and says is designed to bring the best out of her, dressing her in dazzling white silk, radiant with holiness. And that is how husbands ought to love their wives. They're really doing themselves a favor—since they're already "one" in marriage.
>
> Ephesians 5:25-28 (MSG)

The Lord wants to bestow His love on us. As mentioned in the previous verse, that a husband should evoke our beauty. Isn't that amazing? Some of us need to get with the Lord and just allow Him to flood us with His love and reveal His characteristics so that we could recognize what a healthy relationship looks like by getting to know just how much we mean to Him. When

WEAR THAT CROWN, GIRL

we know how much we mean to Him, then we start behaving accordingly. When we have a healthy relationship with the Lord, He teaches us how to recognize the person who is ours. On the flip side, if we do not know ourselves or how to value ourselves, then we can end up settling. We have all seen relationships where one person ends up being with someone, and we are all baffled by how that is. Don't be that person! Know your worth, you were bought with a high price, and the person that Lord has for you will recognize that price tag and treat you the same way.

I know the season of singleness can be lonely at times, and this is normal. Even people who are married or in relationships feel lonely some or even most of the time. The point of the story is, it's normal to experience this, but if you feel this daily (single or married), then ask yourself why that is, and bring it to the Lord. As believers, we are never alone—we have God always with us. Do you know Him? Start dialoguing with Him so He can fill you up with His presence. Also, check yourself to see if your basic needs are being met for intimacy, relationships, or connection? If they are not, then find friends or family that you can be close with. Therefore, community is important as part of a believer's life. We are not meant to live on an island on our own. We were created for relationships. Even when God created the world, He designed it and said, "It is not good for man to be alone" (Genesis 2:18). We need people to do life with, to share our struggles, pray together, lift each other up. If you do not have a community, ask the Father to help you find it. Believe with your heart as you wait and seek.

Reflection Questions:
- Have you ever settled in your past relationships?
- If so, how did you find out?
- How will you know if he is yours from the Lord?

Overcoming Temptations

We all, at some point of our life, can be overcome by temptation. Temptations can vary from one person to another. You can be more susceptible to food, shopping, gambling, gaming, pornography, or lust. You may even be addicted to something that I have not written here. Either way, the Bible tells us that each person is lured away by their own desires, or rather, it begins with a desire at first and afterward, gives birth to sin,

> When tempted, no one should say, "God is tempting me." For God cannot be tempted by evil, nor does he tempt anyone; but each person is tempted when they are dragged away by their own evil desire and enticed. Then, after desire has conceived, it gives birth to sin; and sin, when it is full-grown, gives birth to death.
>
> James 1:13-15

The reason addictions are bad is because God wants us to be devoted to Him in mind, body, spirit, and soul to Him (2 Corinthians 7:1). He wants us to be free from sin or bondage. Addictions have the same meaning as bondage. When you are addicted to something, you are enslaved to it. But Jesus paid the price for our sin so we would not be slaves to sin. Sin contaminates our spirit with darkness. Addictions are created when the neurological pathways in our brains are imprinted on our psyches, and therefore, they need that stimulus to get that high. These stimuli can be certain images that are cravings that are imprinted on our neurons. But the high only lasts for a while, so over time, you build a tolerance and need a bigger high or

So, if we can recognize our triggers or where we get our pleasures from, then it can be easier to navigate through the temptations that come our way.

STEP 1: Identify your triggers. In other words, what is your cycle of arousal? For example, you wake up, and then you come across the stimuli or your desire through your five senses: sight, hearing, taste, touch, or smell.

STEP 2: The battle starts in the mind or in our thoughts. You are exposed to the stimulus, and next, you are thinking about it. For example, if I have a food addiction, I am thinking about food and visualizing it, imagining, etc. Once we imagine it or think about it, we have two directions this is going to play out if the opportunity presents itself. We can indulge our desires, or we can run from our desires. This is how sin works. Either our sin masters us, or we master our sin.

I want to remind you that there is hope. We can turn to our Jesus, who is our Savior who overcame sin and who has the power to forgive sin if we confess and repent. The Bible tells us to resist the devil, and he will flee. So, it seems easy, I know, but practically to apply it is harder than it sounds. Jesus models how He overcame the enemy when He was tempted in the wilderness (Matthew) by replying, "It is written..." There is nothing more powerful than the Word of God. You can't argue with it. So, therefore, fill yourself with the Word of God, it is life, and that life will overflow through you as well. Other things that help are getting into the presence of God through worship music or fellowship with other believers. What happens when we step into the light? It exposes our darkness and sin. So, when we are in the presence of God Almighty, and we start worshiping Him and bowing down to Him, we begin to get empowered by His presence or through encounters with Him.

Even if you did engage in sin or temptations, there is hope. Come to Him who can clean you up and create a new beginning for you. Sin brings upon us shame or guilt, and the last thing we want to do is to confess it to someone but do the opposite—run to the light. Ask other strong believers to pray with you and keep you accountable. You don't have to fight this temptation on your own. In isolation is where we are more susceptible to the enemy, so seek help from the Lord and other strong Christians. Remember, there is no condemnation for those that are in Christ Jesus (Romans 8:1).

Sometimes we are more afraid of what others are going to think about our sin instead of what God thinks about our sin. Who cares what others think of you? They have their own stuff that they need to be concerned about. At the end of your life, it's not going to matter what others think about you, but what God thinks about you. Do not let the enemy in your mind, he is sly and, therefore, begins to appease your senses by subtle questioning, "Did God really say that?" Or "Just try it, and you'll see." Sin begins with desire, and once that desire is grown, it is conceived to sin. The enemy's job is to kill, steal, and destroy. But Jesus came to give life and life with abundance (John 10:10, AMP). So, if what you are involved in is not giving you life, then run to Jesus, who is the way, the truth, and the life (John 14:6). Don't be misled and settle for crumbs or bondage.

Reflect on your life; what are common temptations in your life? How can you start dismantling them, practically? Maybe there are certain places that you should not visit or put certain restrictions on your electronic device. Also, do not give a green light to the enemy. Stand firm before Him, with your prayer and scripture, so he can flee (James 4:7). The Bible says that if we feed our spiritual man, then he will be the one in charge, but if we feed our impulses or physical desires, then our body will be in charge. Those who live according to the flesh have their minds set on what the flesh desires, but those who live in accordance with the Spirit have their minds set on what the Spirit desires (Romans 8:5).

"You, my brothers and sisters, were called to be free. But do not use your freedom to indulge the flesh; rather, serve one another humbly in love."

Galatians 5:13

"So I say, walk by the Spirit, and you will not gratify the desires of the flesh."

Galatians 5:16

"But the fruit of the Spirit is love, joy, peace, forbearance, kindness, goodness, faithfulness, self-control."

Galatians 5:22

Reflection Questions:

- What areas of weaknesses do you possess?
- What are your triggers when it comes to being tempted?

Are They a Distraction or Are They from the Lord?

The person who we are meant to be with will come with peace and God's hand upon the orchestration of your unity. Nothing will be forced by each of you, so it will be effortless for the relationship to work out, for we know that God's blessing brings joy and no sorrow (Proverbs 10:22, AMP). When I was younger, I would always be like, "God, is this guy mine? Cause he is so cute." And afterward, I would come up with a list of ideas of how this could work between us. At times, I would even have dreams about the crushes or believe that the crush was from the Lord. They were not, and I was confused when it did not work out. But there will be no confusion with the person that the Lord has for you.

I know that the enemy can sometimes twist things to confuse us into thinking someone is going to be ours when they are not. The way you can test it out is by asking yourself if that person likes you (in a romantic way) and if they are pursuing you (if you are the lady). If you have "hinted" or were receptive toward your crush by communicating your interest in them afterward, surrender him to the Lord, even if you had a dream or "dreams" about your crush and are wondering if they are from the Lord. The answer still remains the same, if he is not asking you out or pursuing you, then the enemy is trying to distract you or confuse you, but confusion is not from God. If the person is yours, he is not going to go anywhere, and if he is not, then it's best to guard your heart now before it becomes attached, and then it will be much, much harder or painful.

One Sunday, I was at church, and during service, I heard an audible voice that this one particular guy was going to be my husband. Obviously, I was surprised and, at the same time, wondering what that meant. I went home after that service and was still thinking of what I heard earlier, so I mentioned it to my dad. His response was, "Did the guy approach you or anything?" And I was like, "Nope." And he was like, "Well then, it was not from God then." And he was right. The guy and I never got together, but I did have a crush on him for a while, and he was merely a distraction from the Lord more than anything.

In the beginning of dating or courtship, be open to what the Lord is showing you by paying attention to the signs. Ask God to show you who this person is and if he is yours. Be objective, and ask people who know you and him if they think you are meant to be together. Listen to what they are saying about your relationship or your partner. Then take it to the Lord.

Reflection questions:

- How can we recognize if someone is a distraction?
- How do I stay focused on what God called me to instead?

Stewarding Singleness Season

*The grass is not greener on the other side, you just need to
water your own garden.*

During this season that you are in, be intentional
with your time, energy, and relationships. Take the
time to take inventory of your heart and ask God to
show you what is growing in there so far. Your heart is
like a garden, and what you allow to grow inside of it
is what the fruit will produce. You cannot expect good
fruit if you are allowing bitterness or resentment to
take root in your heart. It is our responsibility to guard
our hearts, as the Bible teaches us. This means it's not
your neighbor's, pastor's, or your leader's responsibility, but yours. When the Bible talks about guarding our
hearts, it means to be alert to what our eyes and ears are
listening to or watching. If we are always surrounded
by negativity, fear, or evil, then that is what is coming

WEAR THAT CROWN, GIRL

out in our words and actions. This why the Bible speaks to us about what comes out of our mouths is what was in our hearts (Luke 6:45). So in order for us to have good fruit, it can be spiritual fruit as mentioned in the Bible as love, peace, longsuffering, gentleness, peace, patience, self-control, joy, and kindness (Galatians 5:22-23). Do you see these in your life? If not, then let's start planting them and start praying that the Holy Spirit convicts us of things like gossip, slander, evil, negativity, complaining, and so forth, and helps us to instead start replacing those with good fruit in our lives. What changes may you need to make so you start developing good fruit in your life? It may be to remove some people from your inner circle if they are not influencing you toward good deeds or toward where God is leading you.

If our garden is polluted, then over time, the bad roots will take place and eventually grow up to where it is a garden that is contaminated with weeds in every area of our lives. I have witnessed this with so many people. I had a best friend growing up, and she had a history of lying to other people or gossiping behind other people's backs. We met when we were kids and became best friends when we became teenagers. So when I noticed that she would gossip about others, I started wondering if she was a good influence on me. Soon after that, we grew apart and no longer hung out due to different interests and values. As time went by, this friend could not keep friends. And when we would reconnect to catch up in adulthood, I noticed that she was still the same friend that I had known when she was a teenager. Her bad fruit was still present but only continued to grow larger as she grew older. The patterns were undeniable and toxic, and no matter what I would say, she would just want to gossip and make fun of them. She had a sad life, no true joy, and ended up passing away at a young age due to cancer.

In a season of singleness, this is a time to really get to know ourselves and who we are in Christ. Pray, so the Lord reveals your identity to you. Ask what your giftings are in the body of Christ. Gifts mean whatever comes naturally to you and you enjoy doing. For example, it could be writing, singing, or playing an instrument. The Bible teaches us that the gift makes room for us (Proverbs 18:16, NKJV). That means that we don't have to strive or go out of ourselves to make it happen. It just means that we are faithful with what the Lord has given us, and we are being servants with it. If you do not yet understand your gifting, then you need to start somewhere and try new ministries or explore your passions. And through the process, you will get to know what you enjoy and what you don't. So begin to dream with Him and delight yourself in the Lord. That could be through playing an instrument, creating something, or cooking. Afterward, offer up your gifting to the Lord as you are doing it, as if for Him.

Another amazing thing that happens while you're in the season of singleness is there is so much more to unfold. Some people go through refinement when they're in a relationship, and some people go through refinement before they get into a relationship, but God will never stop working on us. Regardless of where you are in your process, ask the Lord to show you what He is teaching you. Reflect over your life, are there areas in your heart that the Lord wants to heal? Are there any areas in your heart that He wants to uproot, perhaps certain habits, patterns of thinking, or strongholds? A lot of the time, when we see others happy (or we think that they are happy), we can become envious. However, God is an impartial God. He does not have favorites, and He cannot go against His Word. We all get opportunities in life, we might not have the ability to change our ethnicity or where we grew up, but we all get the opportunity to be faithful with the talents and gifts that He's given us (Matthew). What talent have you buried? Is there a dream in your heart that God wants to resurrect? If so, identify what the dream or the gift is in your life and be faithful with that. Invest your time and energy by serving the Lord with all your heart. In your singleness season, this is the time for it. We sometimes forget that in our season of singleness, we have so much more time and focus that we can dedicate to the Lord because we seek to please Him only. However, once we are married, our priorities shift a little bit as Peter writes in the New Testament, "We're not only concerned about the Lord but also about pleasing our husbands or wives" (1 Corinthians 7:33).

We might not see it with our eyes right now, the glory that's coming and the praises to our Lord, but be prepared and assured that the Lord is faithful with each of His words. And He can do the miraculous, He can do the unthinkable, and He can do the supernatural. The deader or outdated we are, the more the Lord has room to shine. Because when all hope has been lost, that's when the Lord is going to step in at the right time. So open up your desires before the Lord because He is looking forward to fulfilling them.

Jesus came to bring us life and life with abundance (John 10:10, ESV). Ask yourself, "Am I living out the fullness that Christ came to give?" If not, then pray for more in your life. Seek Him out and invite Him into every area of your life so He can be Lord. Surrender all to His feet, and you'll taste and see how good the Lord is. Lastly, keep praying and believing for your future spouse. Afterward, follow the Lord's leading so He will lead you to your man. Be open to the people who you come across but guard your heart until the Lord reveals who is meant to be your partner. Give your desires to the Lord, and ask Him to mold you, shape you, into who He planned ahead of time and the same with your future spouse.

Ask yourself if you are single, "Am I happy with myself?" This means with your character, living by yourself, or maybe with being single, with where you are at in life. Do you have peace with yourself, God, your family, and others? If not, then that is a good place to start. If we are not a happy single, we are not going to be happily married because after the emotions of the honeymoon stage wear off; then life will go back to normal with responsibilities, work, and daily life. The issues that were there before you got married will still be there after you are married, but now you have another person next to you who has their own stuff that needs to be dealt with. In a way, it's nice to have someone near, but at the same time, the issues are still there. So, find out what motivates you? What inspires you? What are your triggers? We all have patterns of thinking and/or habits, so get to know yourself and who you are, and what you like and do not like. If you throw a pity party often, maybe that is a sign that there is some work that needs to be done, so you are comfortable with yourself and are in a place to bring something to the table.

I was reminded of how the home that I live in right now, how perfect it is in every way for me, and how I came across it. A few months before I moved into it,

I was shopping around the neighborhood and came across where I live now. I fell in love with the home and the area, and I remember just saying to the Lord I'd love to live somewhere like that. It's so beautiful; it's everything I've ever wanted. I forgot my prayer and went on with my life, forgetting about the home. The Lord reminded me, after I moved in, that the very thing that I was dreaming about and shared with the Lord is the very thing that the Lord granted. And that was just my home living situation. Imagine what He will do with our future spouses. It's going to be mind-blowing. It's going to be like that verse, no man has seen, no ear has heard what the Lord has prepared for those that love Him. Do you believe Him? Praise the Lord!

Reflection Questions:
- What fruit have I been producing in my life?
- What is holding me back from living my fullest life with Jesus?

Conclusion

I hope this book has encouraged you in your singleness season. There is something significant and beautiful in every season, so may the Lord continue to use it for His glory. I am believing with you that every promise still stands regarding my future husband and yours, and it will be fulfilled in His timing. Meanwhile, I am continuing to trust Him that He has every detail figured out, and we can rest in Him. May all the distractions and all that do not bring Him glory be blown away in Jesus' name. Let's fix our eyes on the Author of our faith, Jesus. Lovely one, you are royal, so wear that crown confidently, do not settle for crumbs. You are dreamed up and placed here on earth by our Heavenly Father. You are not a mistake; you have a purpose. Remember, you are never alone, and even if you feel like it at times, remember our Heavenly Father is always with us (Deuteronomy 31:6).

With love, blessings!

Book Description

This book was on your Father's heart for you! The topics were inspired by Him and written to see His daughters understand the love and purpose He has for His daughters. In the book, I dive deeper to explore how sometimes our association to wanting to get married is tied to our happiness. The desire to get married is not wrong or anything and I believe is God's desire for His daughters. The book reveals the lies that we have come to believe that if we meet our partner, then we can live happily ever after. Nobody can really make us truly happy and meet all of our needs because that is not God's plan. Our satisfaction can only be found in Christ alone. This book shows how to thrive in your singleness season by understanding your royal identity as a daughter of a King.

Wear That Crown, Girl is an encouraging book that is relatable to all the singles out there. It is filled with raw stories, testimonies, and the struggles for singles. It provides the space to relate and find encouragement in their singleness season. The book was inspired by the Lord, and I felt the Father's heart for the ladies as I was writing the book. The Father wanted the ladies to know that they are created *by God* and *for God* that has amazing plans for them, and He wants to reveal His plans and identify their worth to them.

About the Author

Anna Pavlov is an Associate Marriage and Family Therapist. She helps individuals find freedom and healing from depression, anxiety, trauma by understanding their identity through Christ. Anna also has been a guest speaker at a few different women's ministries as well as lead women's bible study groups and part of different ministries over the past ten years and enjoys traveling, teaching, and starting off her morning with coffee and God's Word.

CPSIA information can be obtained
at www.ICGtesting.com
Printed in the USA
FSHW020915250521
81644FS

9 781637 693308